Bobby Bro Cat

written by **Elizabeth Pulford**
illustrated by Daniel J Brown

Bobby Brown was new in town.

"I don't like it here,"
Bobby said to his mum.
"I don't have any friends."

"I have a friend for you,"
smiled Mum.

"Come with me."

Mum and Bobby went
into the kitchen.
On the floor was a big brown box.

SCRATCH! SCRATCH!

What was inside the box?

"Is it a puppy?" asked Bobby.

Mum smiled.
"Open the lid and find out,"
she said.

Bobby opened the lid,
and peeped inside.
He saw a big grey cat.

"*Purr! Purr!*" said the big grey cat.

At dinner time, the *purring* stopped.

"Where's the big grey cat?"
said Bobby.
"I miss the big grey cat.
I miss its *purr, purr, purr.*"

So Bobby looked all around the house
for the big grey cat.
He looked in every cupboard
and under every chair.
He looked behind the cushions
and under the table.
But he didn't find the big grey cat.

"*Purr! Purr! Purr!*"

"What was that?" said Bobby.

He looked in his bed.
The big grey cat was
under his covers, fast asleep.

"I don't want a puppy," said Bobby.
"I want a cat."

The big grey cat slowly opened
one eye and *purred*.